the metal album
play guitar w

CW00500744

black sabbath, metallica, guns n' roses, ac/dc, def leppard and bon jovi

12.99

Wise Publications
London/New York/Paris/Sydney/Copenhagen/Madrid

Exclusive Distributors:
Music Sales Limited
8/9 Frith Street,
London W1V 5TZ, England.
Music Sales Pty Limited
120 Rothschild Avenue,
Rosebery, NSW 2018,
Australia.

Order No. AM954426
ISBN 0-7119-7250-8
This book © Copyright 1999 by Wise Publications

Compiled by Peter Evans
Music arranged by Arthur Dick
Music processed by Andrew Shiels
Cover design by Studio Twenty, London
Photographs courtesy of London Features International

Printed in the United Kingdom by
Caligraving Limited, Thetford, Norfolk.

CD programmed by John Moores
Tracks 5 & 13 recorded by Andy Spiller
Tracks 2, 3, 10 & 11 recorded by Passionhouse Music
Tracks 4, 9, 12 & 17 recorded by Kester Sims
All guitars by Arthur Dick
(except Tracks 6, 8, 14 & 16, by Martin Shellard)
With special thanks to Andy Milner at Marshall for supply of amplification

Your Guarantee of Quality
As publishers, we strive to produce every book to the
highest commercial standards.
The music has been carefully designed to minimise awkward
page turns and to make playing from it a real pleasure.
Particular care has been given to specifying acid-free,
neutral-sized paper made from pulps which have not been
elemental chlorine bleached. This pulp is from farmed
sustainable forests and was produced with special
regard for the environment.
Throughout, the printing and binding have been planned
to ensure a sturdy, attractive publication which should
give years of enjoyment.
If your copy fails to meet our high standards,
please inform us and we will gladly replace it.

www.playguitarwith.com
www.musicsales.co.uk

Music Sales' complete catalogue describes thousands of titles
and is available in full colour sections by subject, direct from
Music Sales Limited. Please state your areas of interest
and send a cheque/postal order for £1.50 for postage to:
Music Sales Limited, Newmarket Road,
Bury St. Edmunds, Suffolk IP33 3YB.

guitar tablature explained

Guitar music can be notated three different ways: on a musical stave, in tablature, and in rhythm slashes

RHYTHM SLASHES are written above the stave. Strum chords in the rhythm indicated. Round noteheads indicate single notes.

THE MUSICAL STAVE shows pitches and rhythms and is divided by lines into bars. Pitches are named after the first seven letters of the alphabet.

TABLATURE graphically represents the guitar fingerboard. Each horizontal line represents a string, and each number represents a fret.

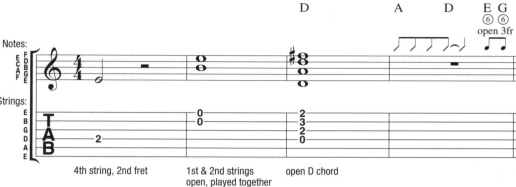

4th string, 2nd fret

1st & 2nd strings open, played together

open D chord

definitions for special guitar notation

SEMI-TONE BEND: Strike the note and bend up a semi-tone (1/2 step).

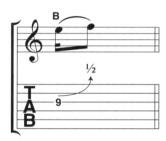

WHOLE-TONE BEND: Strike the note and bend up a whole-tone (whole step).

GRACE NOTE BEND: Strike the note and bend as indicated. Play the first note as quickly as possible.

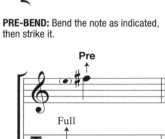

QUARTER-TONE BEND: Strike the note and bend up a 1/4 step.

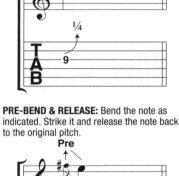

BEND & RELEASE: Strike the note and bend up as indicated, then release back to the original note.

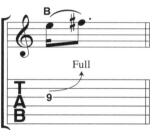

BEND & RESTRIKE: Strike the note and bend as indicated then restrike the string where the symbol occurs.

PRE-BEND: Bend the note as indicated, then strike it.

PRE-BEND & RELEASE: Bend the note as indicated. Strike it and release the note back to the original pitch.

HAMMER-ON: Strike the first (lower) note with one finger, then sound the higher note (on the same string) with another finger by fretting it without picking.

PULL-OFF: Place both fingers on the notes to be sounded. Strike the first note and without picking, pull the finger off to sound the second (lower) note.

LEGATO SLIDE (GLISS): Strike the first note and then slide the same fret-hand finger up or down to the second note. The second note is not struck.

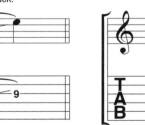

SHIFT SLIDE (GLISS & RESTRIKE): Same as legato slide, except the second note is struck.

NATURAL HARMONIC: Strike the note while the fret-hand lightly touches the string directly over the fret indicated.

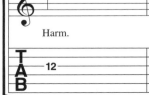

PICK SCRAPE: The edge of the pick is rubbed down (or up) the string, producing a scratchy sound.

PALM MUTING: The note is partially muted by the pick hand lightly touching the string(s) just before the bridge.

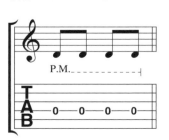

MUFFLED STRINGS: A percussive sound is produced by laying the fret hand across the string(s) without depressing, and striking them with the pick hand.

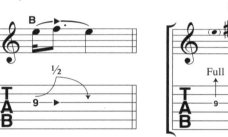

NOTE: The speed of any bend is indicated by the music notation and tempo.

fade to black

Words & Music by James Hetfield, Lars Ulrich, Cliff Burton & Kirk Hammett

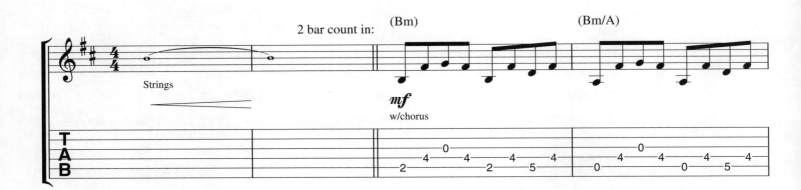

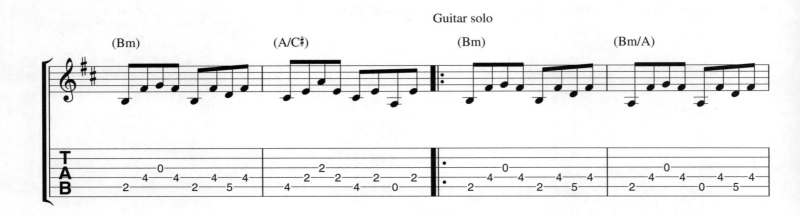

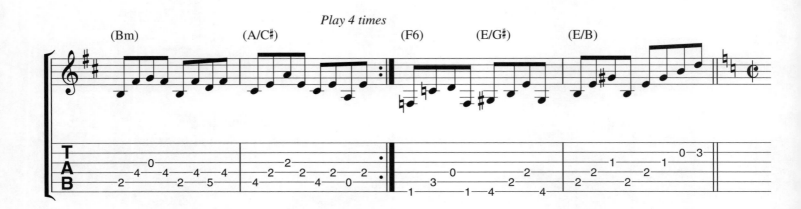

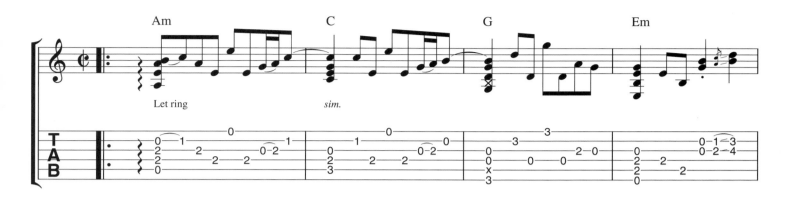

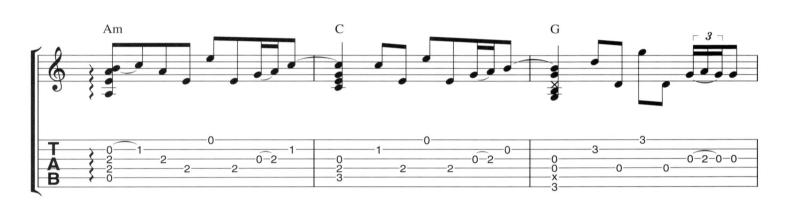

Verse

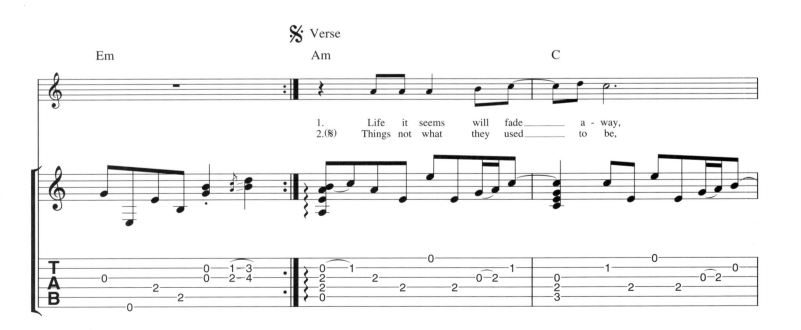

1.   Life it seems   will fade_____ a - way,
2. (𝄋) Things not what   they used_____ to be,

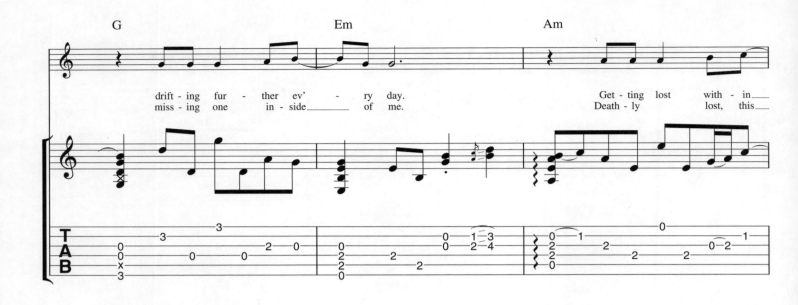

drift - ing fur - ther ev' - ry day.
miss - ing one in - side of me.

Get - ting lost with - in
Death - ly lost, this

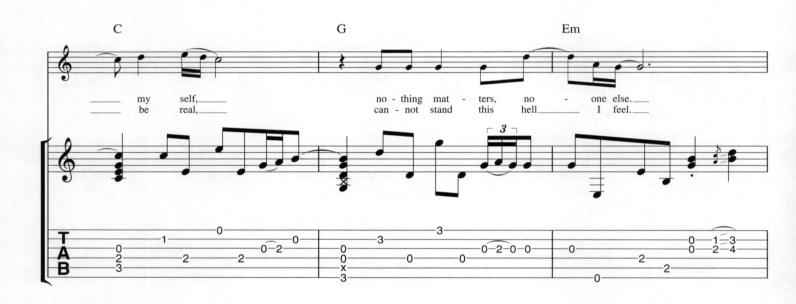

— my self,
— be real,

no - thing mat - ters, no - one else.
can - not stand this hell I feel.

I have lost the will to live,
Emp - ti - ness is fill - ing me,

sim - ply noth - ing more
to the point of ag -

6

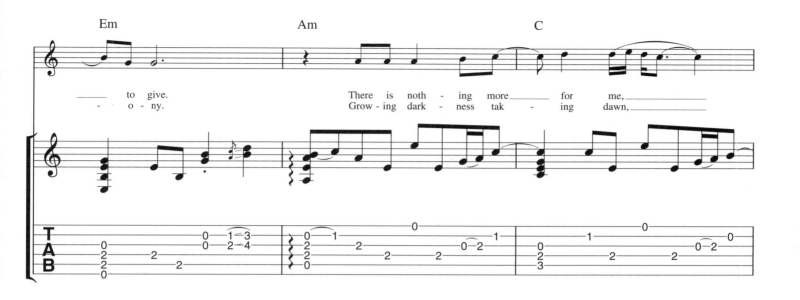

to give.
- - o - ny.

There is noth - ing more_____ for me,_____
Grow - ing dark - ness tak - ing dawn,_____

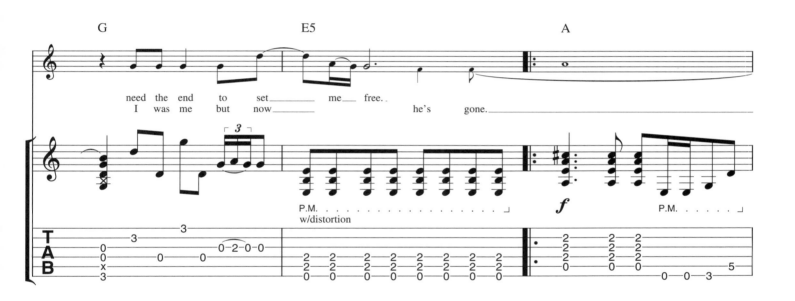

need the end to set_____ me__ free.
I was me but now he's gone._____

P.M. . . . .
w/distortion

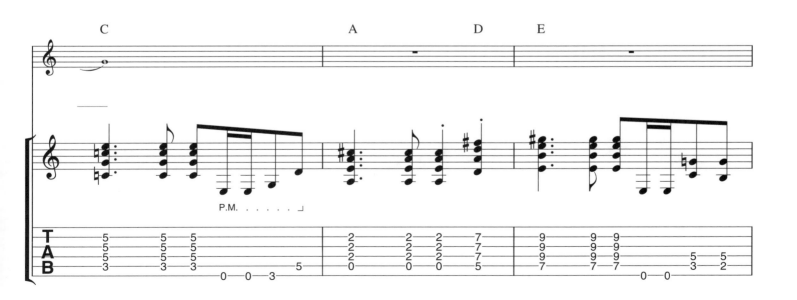

P.M. . . . .

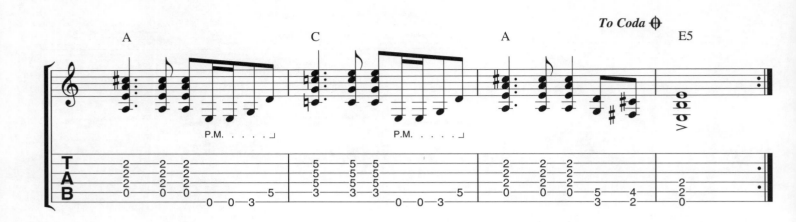

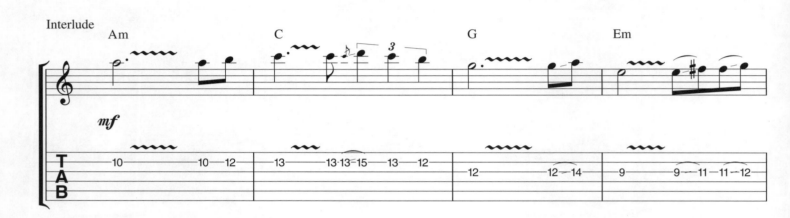

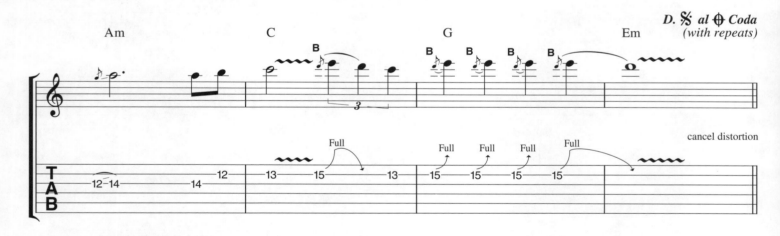

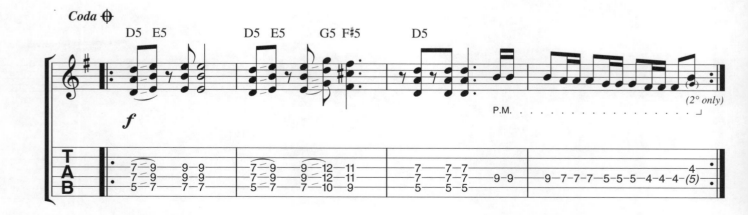

𝄋𝄋 Bridge

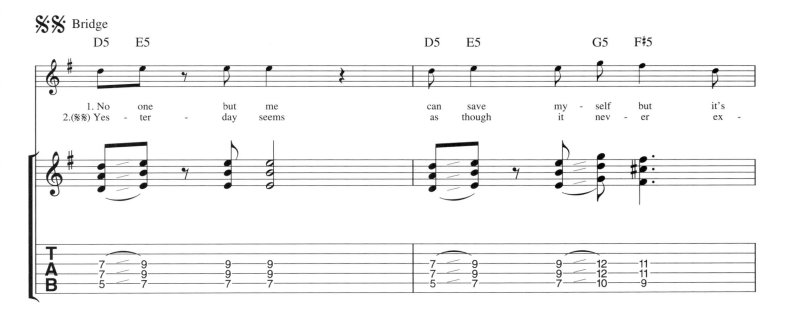

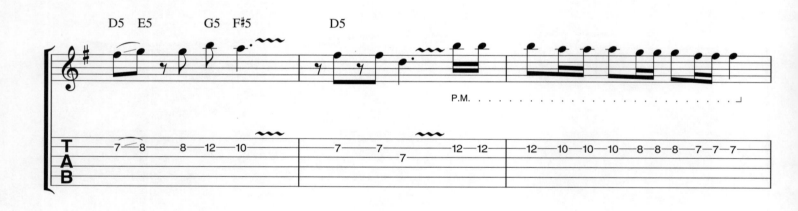

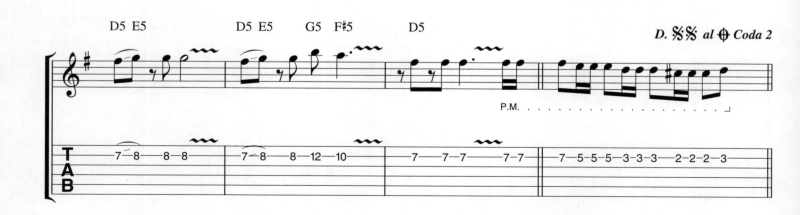

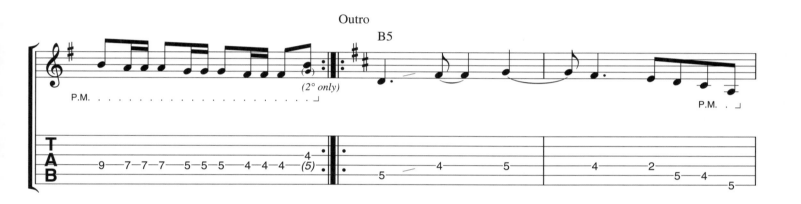

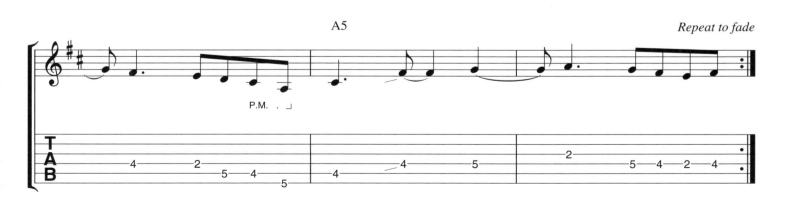

love bites

Words & Music by Steve Clark, Joe Elliott, Rick Savage, Phil Collen & Robert John 'Mutt' Lange

1° & ℅ only, omit 2°

So I don't wan-na be there when you de-cide to break it, no. (Love

Chorus

bites, love bleeds,) it's bring-in' me to my knees. (Love

lives, love dies.) It's no sur-prise, (Love

begs, love pleads,) it's what I need.

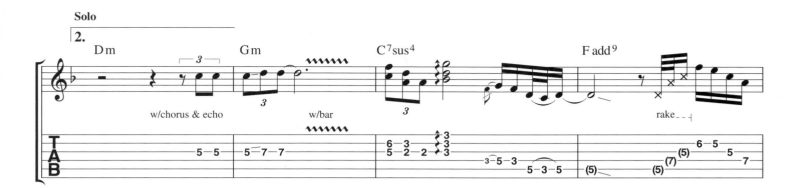

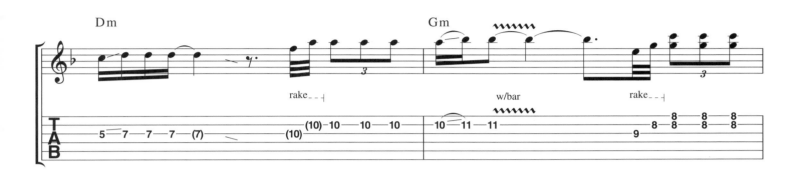

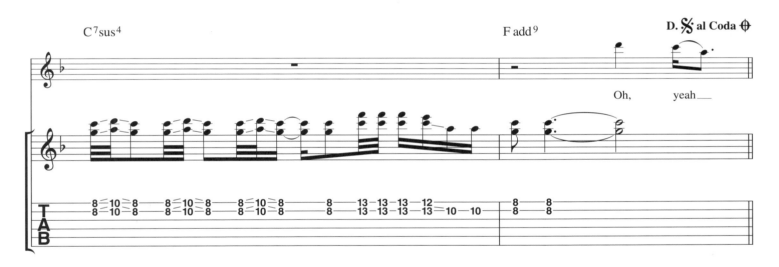

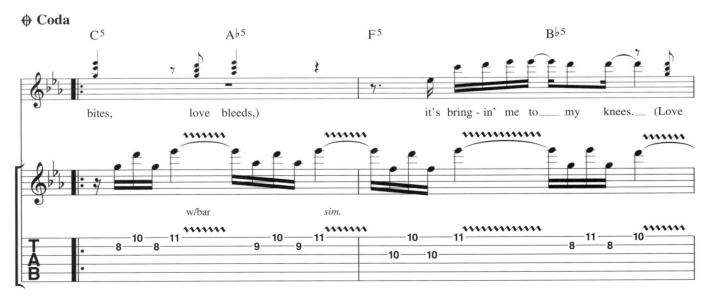

live and let die

Words & Music by Paul & Linda McCartney

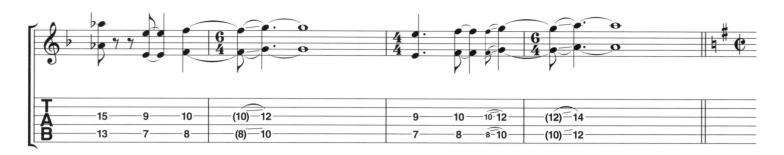

Bridge
Half tempo, Reggae feel

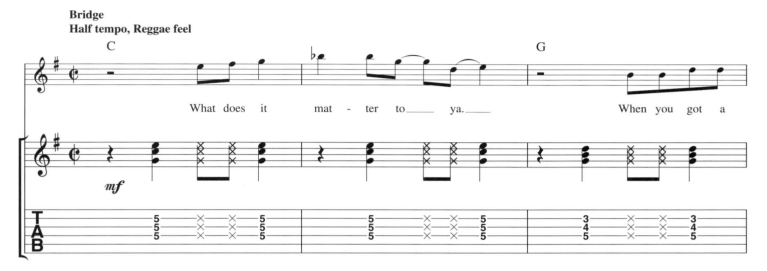

What does it mat - ter to ya. When you got a

job to do, ya got to do it well. You got to

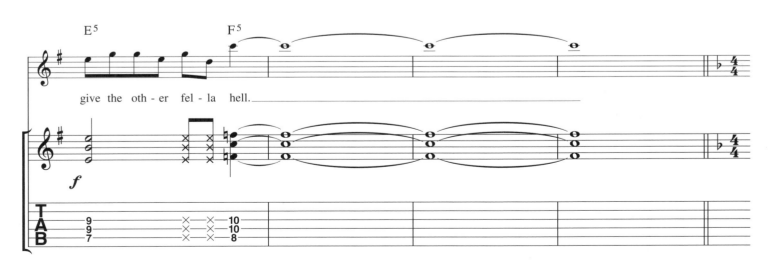

give the oth - er fel - la hell.

Half tempo

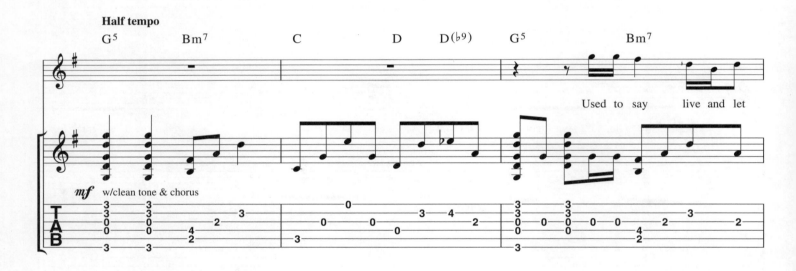

Used to say   live and let

live.___ (You know you did, you know you did, you know you   did.___) But if this ev - er chang - ing world

in which__ we live in__ makes you__ give in and__ cry,__ (ah!) say live and let die.__

Chorus

Live and let die.__

livin' on a prayer

Words & Music by Jon Bon Jovi, Richie Sambora & Desmond Child

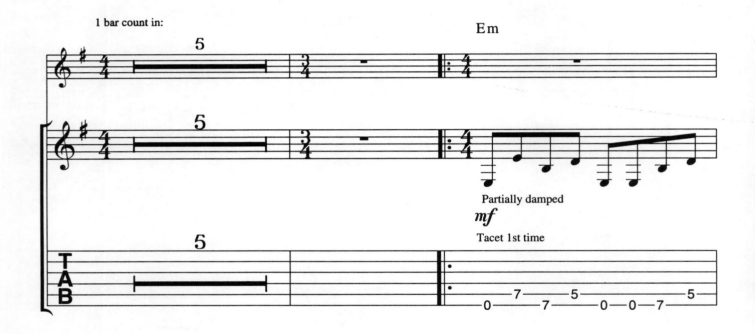

Verse:

1. Tom - my used to work on the docks,_____ Un - ion's been on strike, he's

See Block Lyrics for Verse 2

Tacet 1st time

down on his luck, it's tough,_____ so____ tough.____

Open

Play 1st time

Gi - na works the din - ers all day,

Tacet 1st time

work - in' for her man, she brings home her pay for

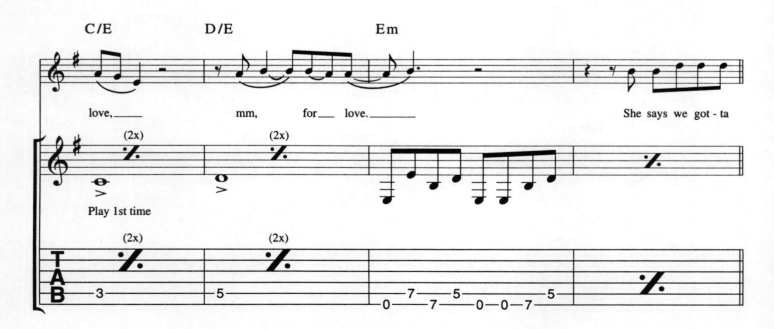

love,____ mm, for____ love.____ She says we got - ta

Play 1st time

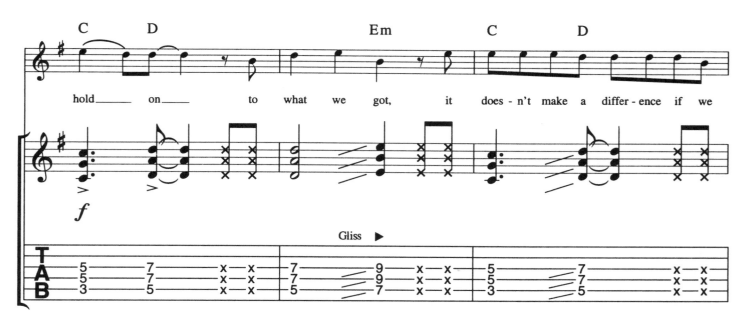

hold____ on____ to what we got, it does-n't make a differ-ence if we

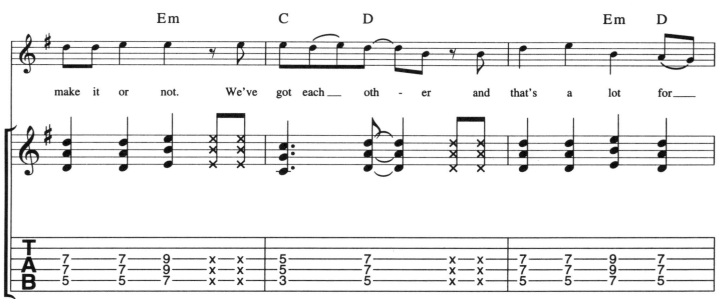

make it or not. We've got each____ oth - er and that's a lot for____

Chorus:

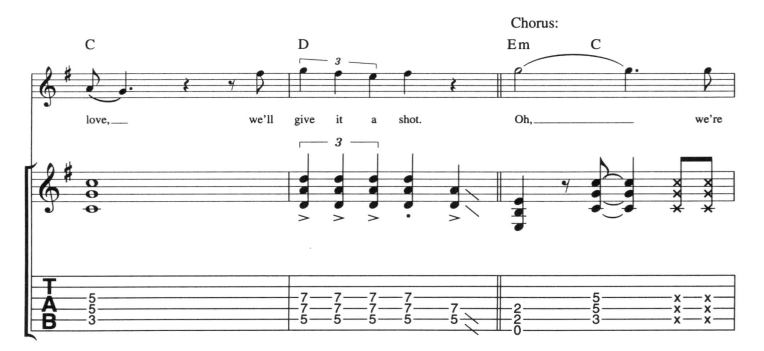

love,____ we'll give it a shot. Oh,_____ we're

Verse 2:
Tommy's got his six string in hock
Now he's holdin' in what he used to make it talk
So tough, mm, it's tough.
Gina dreams of running away
When she cries in the night Tommy whispers
Baby, it's okay, someday.

We've got to hold on *etc.*

paranoid

Words & Music by Terence Butler, John Osbourne, Frank Iommi & William Ward

that make____ true hap - pi - ness,____ I   must be   blind.

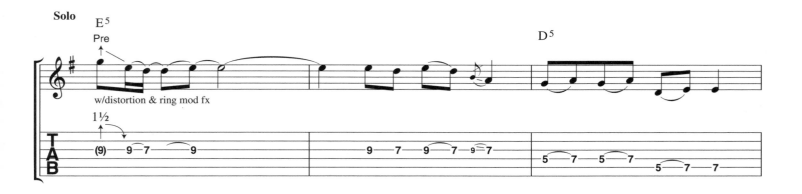

Solo

w/distortion & ring mod fx

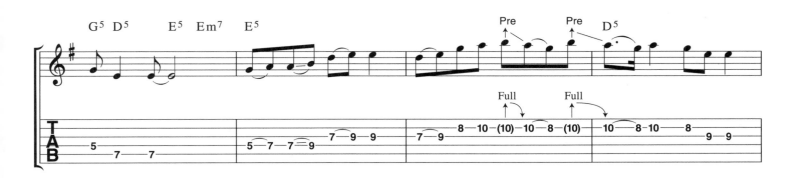

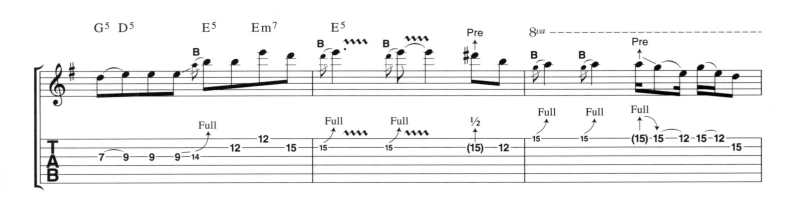

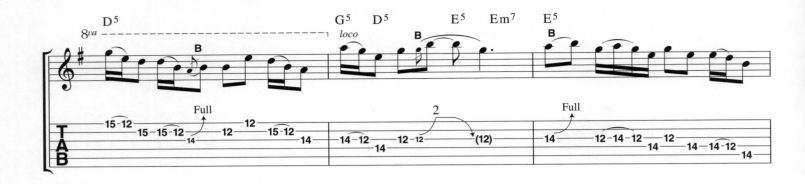

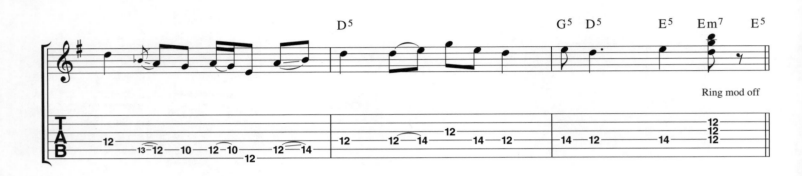

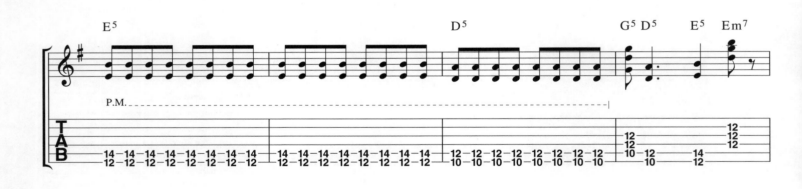

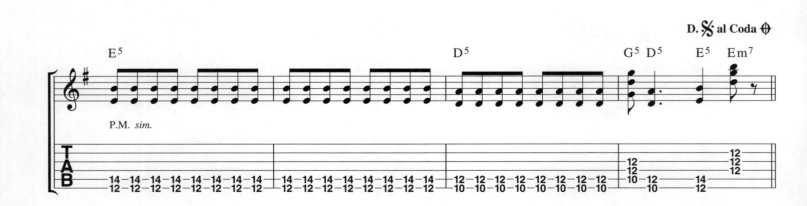

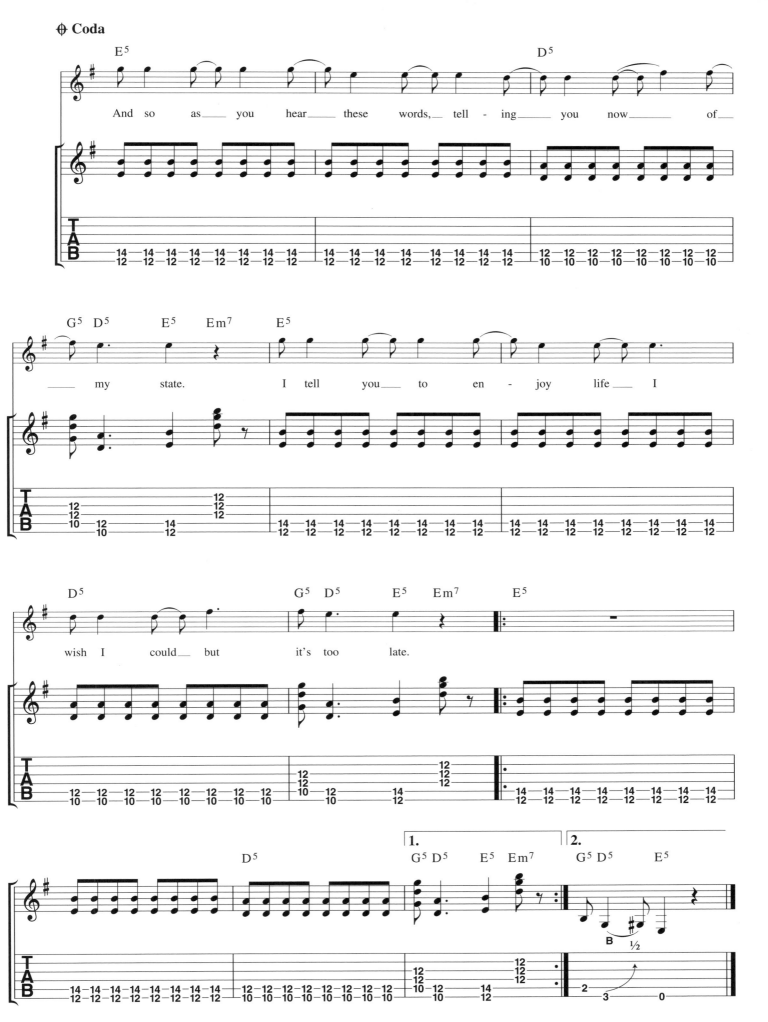

rock and roll ain't noise pollution

Words & Music by Angus Young, Malcolm Young & Brian Johnson

- tion, rock 'n' roll is just rock 'n' roll.

Solo

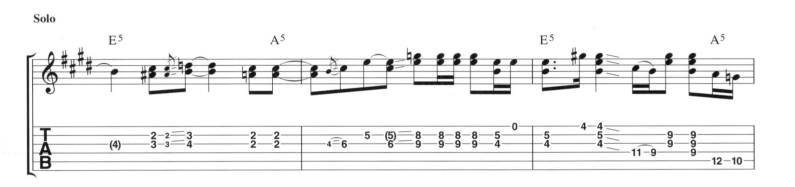

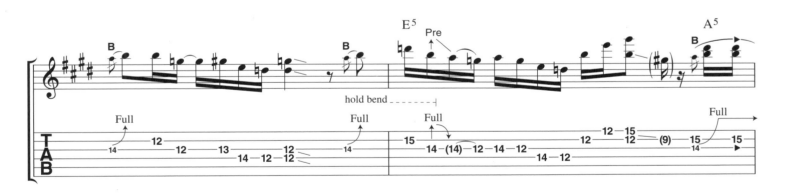

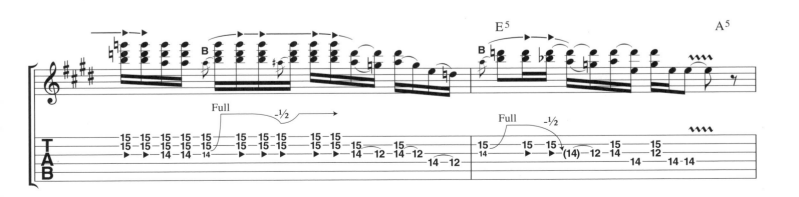

seek and destroy

Words & Music by James Hetfield & Lars Ulrich

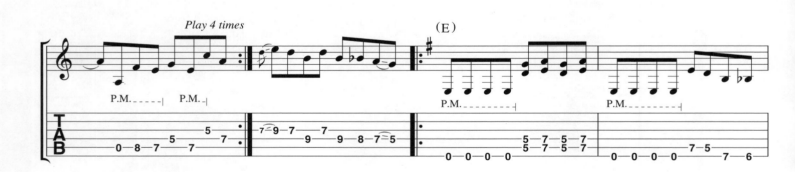

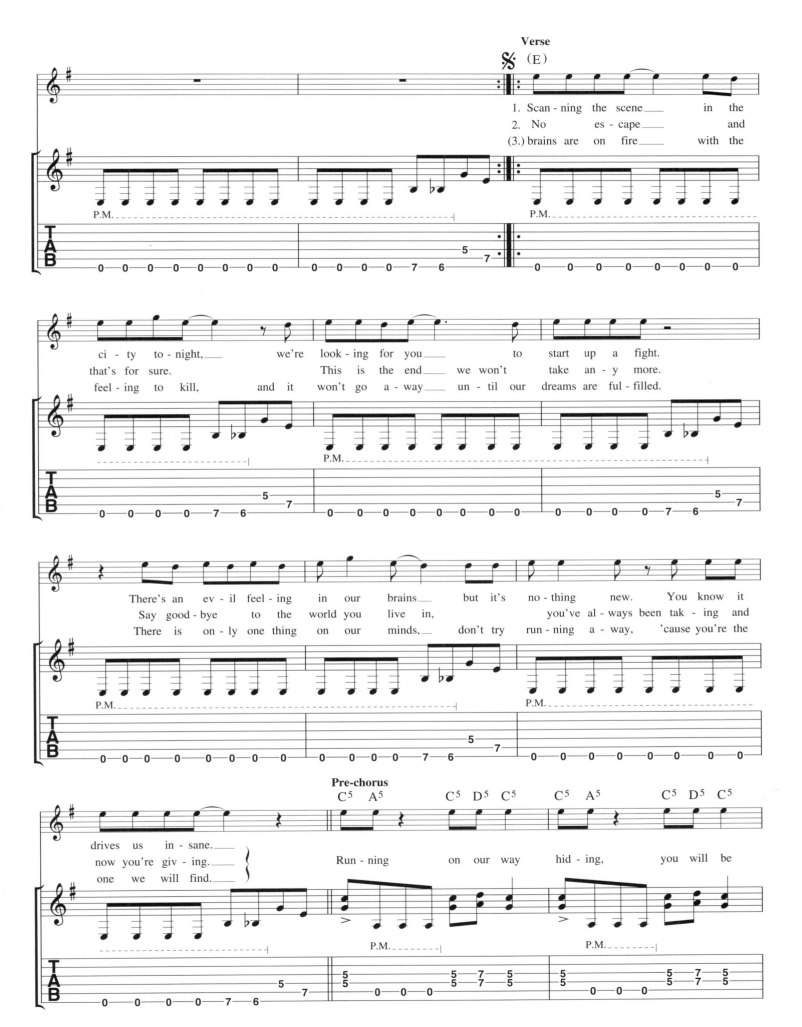

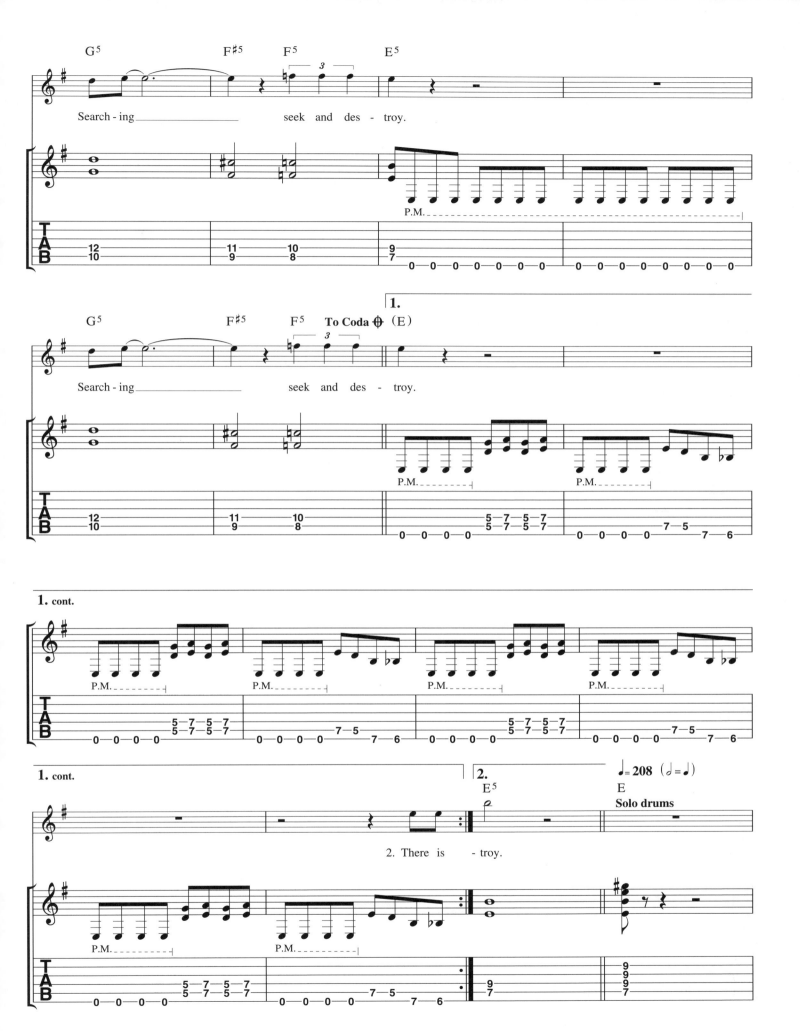

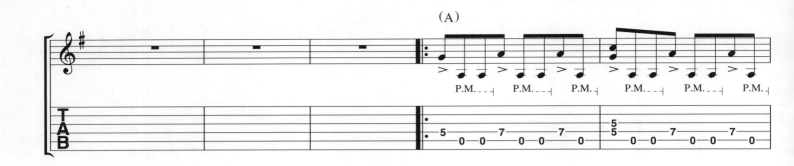

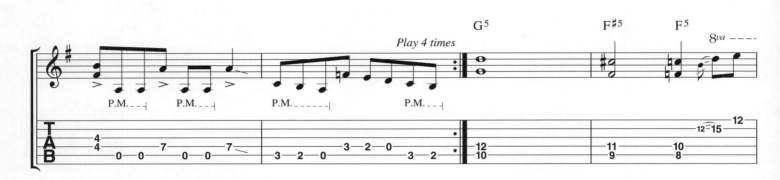

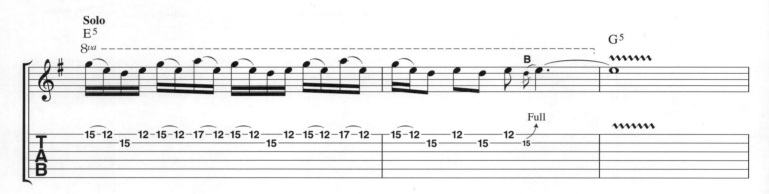

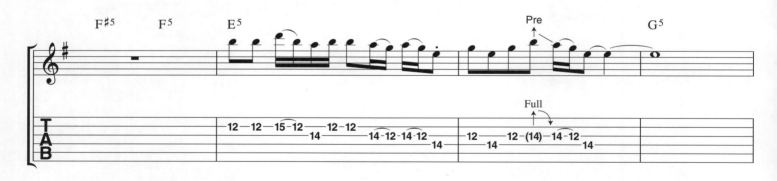

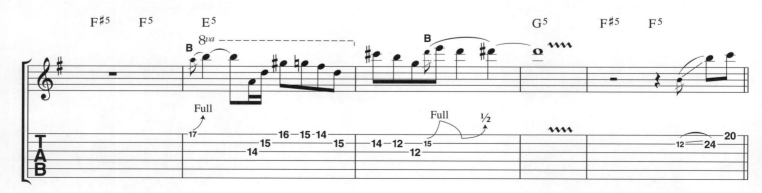

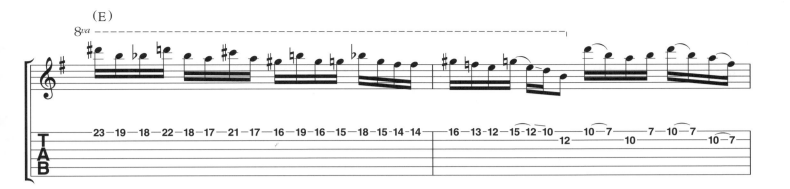

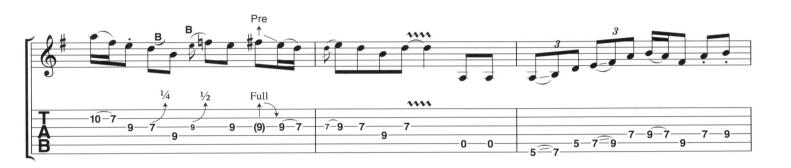

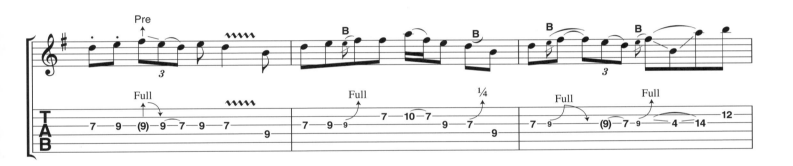

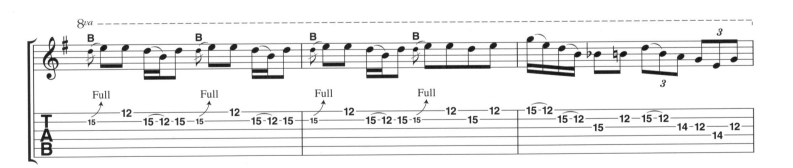

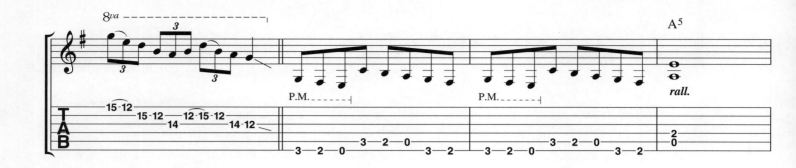

A tempo ♩ = 140

Play 4 times   (E)

2° D. 𝄋 al Coda ⊕

2° only

3. Our -

Coda

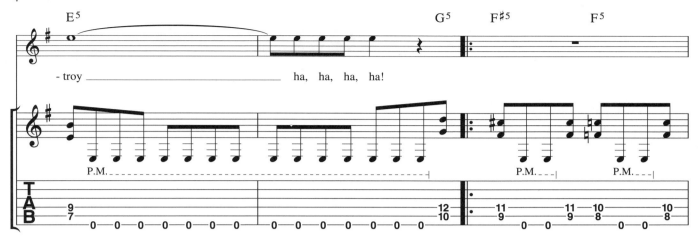

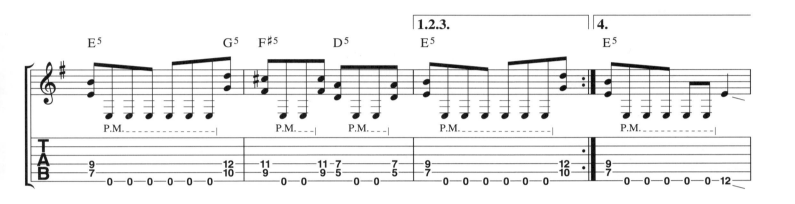

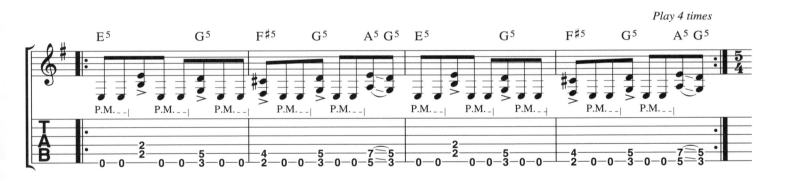

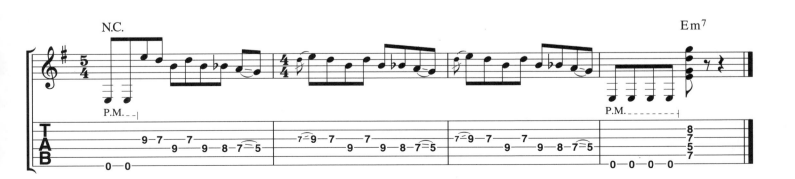

whole lotta rosie

Words & Music by Bon Scott, Angus Young & Malcolm Young

Intro

2 bar count in:

Verse

1. Wan - na tell___ you sto - ry

'bout wom'n I know.___   When it comes___ to lov-

Verse

Chorus

give it all you got,   weigh-in' in at nine-teen   stone.___
to my sur-prise,   huh!   Rosie never stops.

You're a whole lot-ta wom-an,   a whole lot-ta

wom-an,   a whole lot-ta Ros - ie,

whole lot-ta Ros - ie,   a whole lot-ta

Ros - ie,

you're a whole lot - ta wom - an.
1° only

you're a whole lot - ta love.

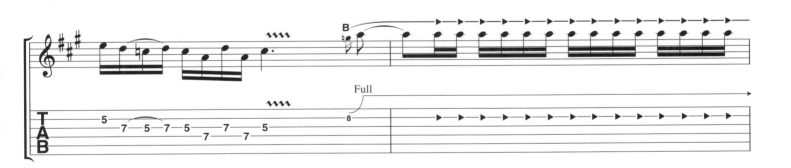
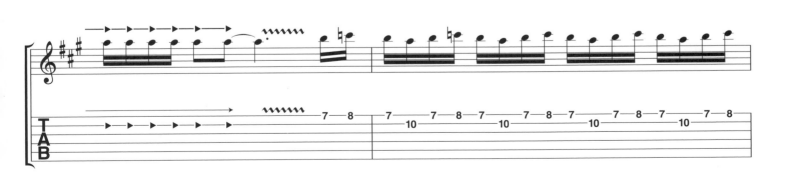

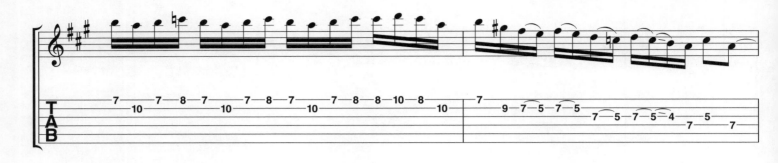

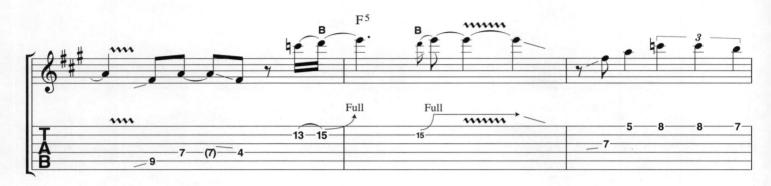

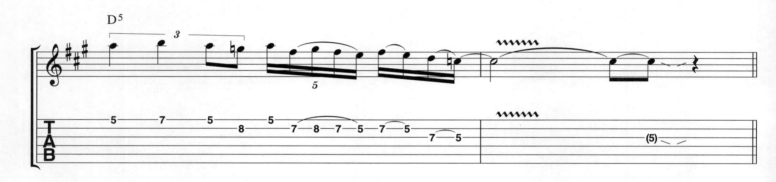

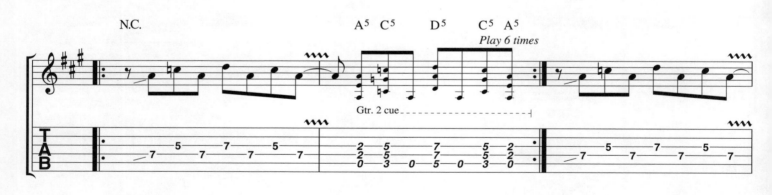

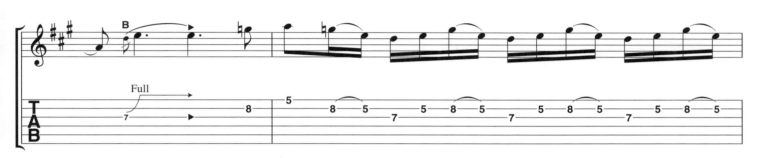

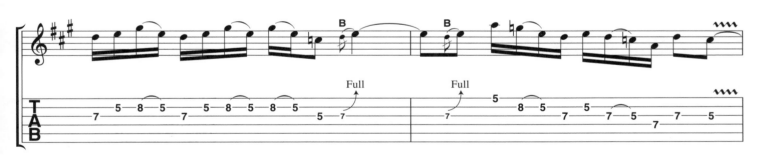

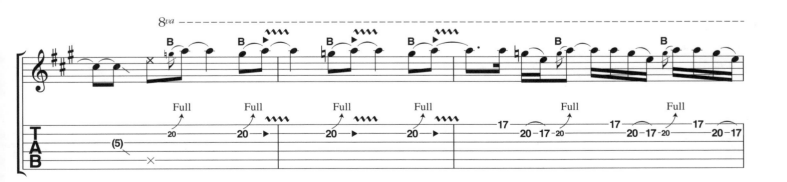

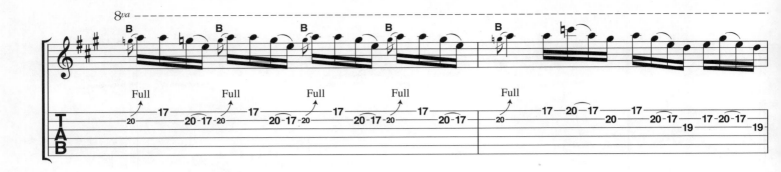

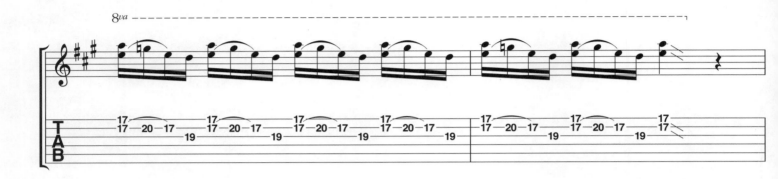

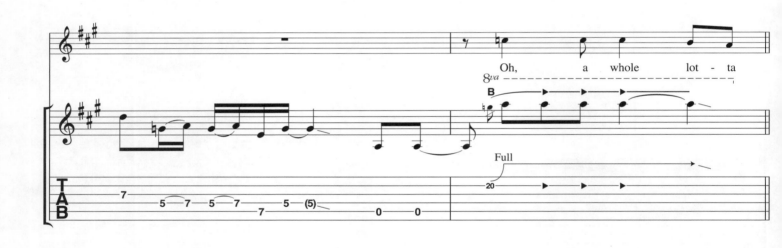

Chorus

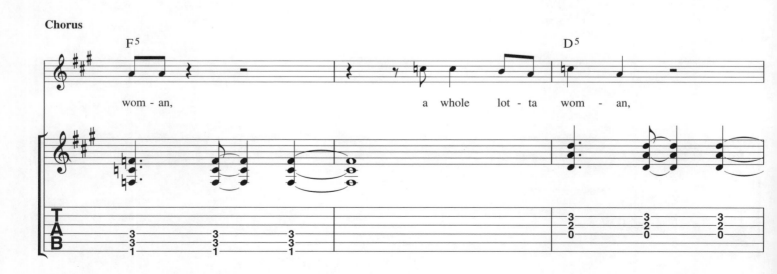

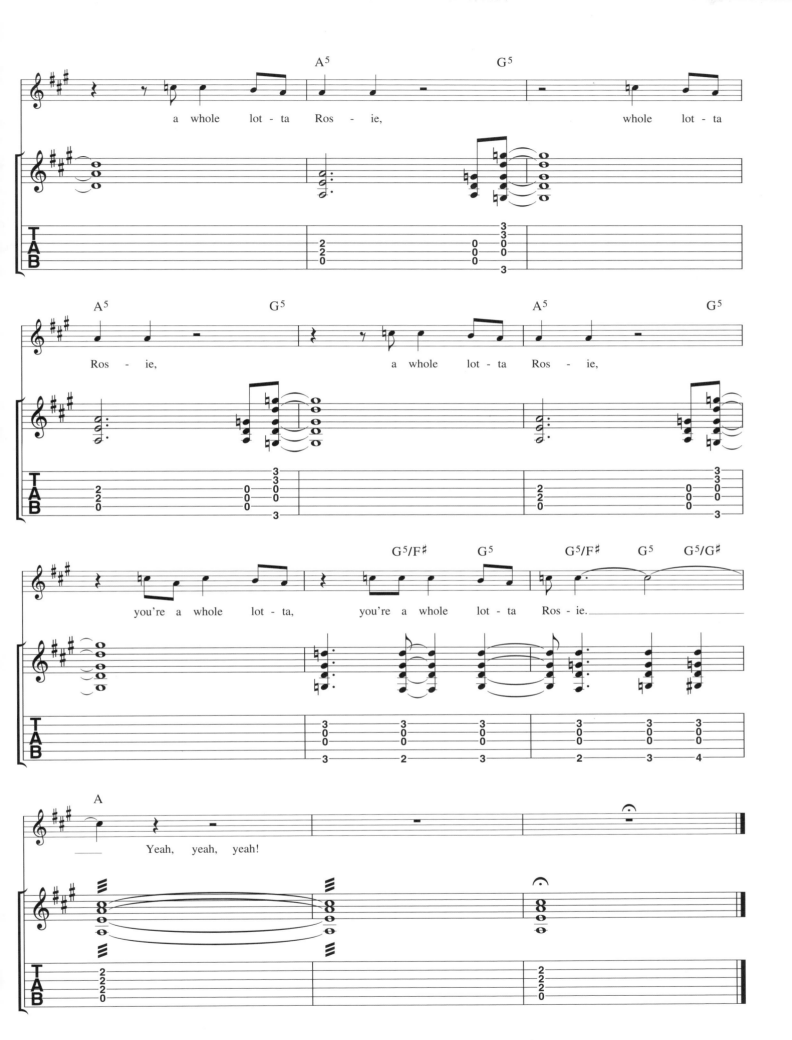

Présentation De La Tablature De Guitare

Il existe trois façons différentes de noter la musique pour guitare : à l'aide d'une portée musicale, de tablatures ou de barres rythmiques.

Les BARRES RYTHMIQUES sont indiquées au-dessus de la portée. Jouez les accords dans le rythme indiqué. Les notes rondes indiquent des notes réciles.

La PORTÉE MUSICALE indique les notes et rythmes et est divisée en mesures. Cette division est représentée par des lignes. Les notes sont : do, ré, mi, fa, sol, la, si.

La PORTÉE EN TABLATURE est une représentation graphique des touches de guitare. Chaque ligne horizontale correspond à une corde et chaque chiffre correspond à une case.

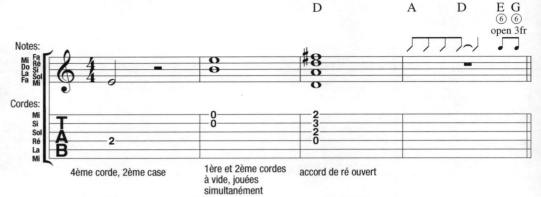

4ème corde, 2ème case — 1ère et 2ème cordes à vide, jouées simultanément — accord de ré ouvert

Notation Spéciale De Guitare : Définitions

TIRÉ DEMI-TON : Jouez la note et tirez la corde afin d'élever la note d'un demi-ton (étape à moitié).

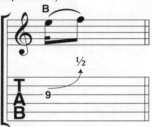

TIRÉ PLEIN : Jouez la note et tirez la corde afin d'élever la note d'un ton entier (étape entière).

TIRÉ D'AGRÉMENT : Jouez la note et tirez la corde comme indiqué. Jouez la première note aussi vite que possible.

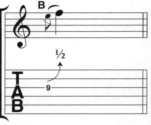

TIRÉ QUART DE TON : Jouez la note et tirez la corde afin d'élever la note d'un quart de ton.

TIRÉ ET LÂCHÉ : Jouez la note et tirez la corde comme indiqué, puis relâchez, afin d'obtenir de nouveau la note de départ.

TIRÉ ET REJOUÉ : Jouez la note et tirez la corde comme indiqué puis rejouez la corde où le symbole apparaît.

PRÉ-TIRÉ : Tirez la corde comme indiqué puis jouez cette note.

PRÉ-TIRÉ ET LÂCHÉ : Tirez la corde comme indiqué. Jouez la note puis relâchez la corde afin d'obtenir le ton de départ.

HAMMER-ON: Jouez la première note (plus basse) avec un doigt puis jouez la note plus haute sur la même corde avec un autre doigt, sur le manche mais sans vous servir du médiator.

PULL-OFF: Positionnez deux doigts sur les notes à jouer. Jouez la première note et sans vous servir du médiator, dégagez un doigt pour obtenir la deuxième note, plus basse.

GLISSANDO : Jouez la première note puis faites glisser le doigt le long du manche pour obtenir la seconde note qui, elle, n'est pas jouée.

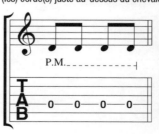

GLISSANDO ET REJOUÉ : Identique au glissando à ceci près que la seconde note est jouée.

HARMONIQUES NATURELLES : Jouez la note tandis qu'un doigt effleure la corde sur le manche correspondant à la case indiquée.

PICK SCRAPE (SCRATCH) : On fait glisser le médiator le long de la corde, ce qui produit un son éraillé.

ÉTOUFFÉ DE LA PAUME : La note est partiellement étouffée par la main (celle qui se sert du médiator). Elle effleure la (les) corde(s) juste au-dessus du chevalet.

CORDES ÉTOUFFÉES : Un effet de percussion produit en posant à plat la main sur le manche sans relâcher, puis en jouant les cordes avec le médiator.

NOTE: La vitesse des tirés est indiquée par la notation musicale et le tempo.

Erläuterung zur Tabulaturschreibweise

Es gibt drei Möglichkeiten, Gitarrenmusik zu notieren: im klassichen Notensystem, in Tabulaturform oder als rhythmische Akzente.

RHYTHMISCHE AKZENTE werden über dem Notensystem notiert. Geschlagene Akkorde werden rhythmisch dargestellt. Ausgeschriebene Noten stellen Einzeltöne dar.

Im **NOTENSYSTEM** werden Tonhöhe und rhythmischer Verlauf festgelegt; es ist durch Taktstriche in Takte unterteilt. Die Töne werden nach den ersten acht Buchstaben des Alphabets benannt.
Beachte: "B" in der anglo-amerkanischen Schreibweise entspricht dem deutschen "H"!

DIE TABULATUR ist die optische Darstellung des Gitarrengriffbrettes. Jeder horizontalen Linie ist eine bestimmte Saite zugeordnet, jede Zahl bezeichnet einen Bund.

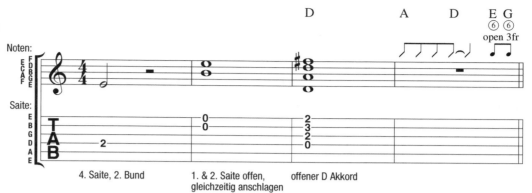

4. Saite, 2. Bund   1. & 2. Saite offen, gleichzeitig anschlagen   offener D Akkord

Erklärungen zur speziellen Gitarennotation

HALBTON-ZIEHER: Spiele die Note und ziehe dann um einen Halbton höher (Halbtonschritt).

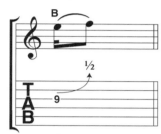

GANZTON-ZIEHER: Spiele die Note und ziehe dann einen Ganzton höher (Ganztonschritt).

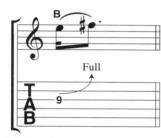

ZIEHER MIT VORSCHLAG: Spiele die Note und ziehe wie notiert. Spiele die erste Note so schnell wie möglich.

VIERTELTON-ZIEHER: Spiele die Note und ziehe dann einen Viertelton höher (Vierteltonschritt).

ZIEHEN UND ZURÜCKGLEITEN: Spiele die Note und ziehe wie notiert; lasse den Finger dann in die Ausgangposition zurückgleiten. Dabei wird nur die erste Note angeschlagen.

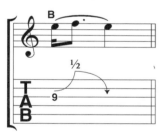

ZIEHEN UND NOCHMALIGES ANSCHLAGEN: Spiele die Note und ziehe wie notiert, schlage die Saite neu an, wenn das Symbol "▶" erscheint und lasse den Finger dann zurückgleiten.

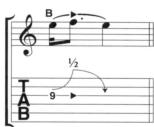

ZIEHER VOR DEM ANSCHLAGEN: Ziehe zuerst die Note wie notiert; schlage die Note dann an.

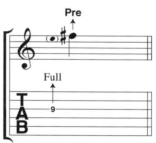

ZIEHER VOR DEM ANSCHLAGEN MIT ZURÜCKGLEITEN: Ziehe die Note wie notiert; schlage die Note dann an und lasse den Finger auf die Ausgangslage zurückgleiten.

AUFSCHLAGTECHNIK: Schlage die erste (tiefere) Note an; die höhere Note (auf der selben Saite) erklingt durch kräftiges Aufschlagen mit einem anderen Finger der Griffhand.

ABZIEHTECHNIK: Setze beide Finger auf die zu spielenden Noten und schlage die erste Note an. Ziehe dann (ohne nochmals anzuschlagen) den oberen Finger der Griffhand seitlich - abwärts ab, um die zweite (tiefere) Note zum klingen zu bringen.

GLISSANDOTECHNIK: Schlage die erste Note an und rutsche dann mit dem selben Finger der Griffhand aufwärts oder abwärts zur zweiten Note. Die zweite Note wird nicht angeschlagen.

GLISSANDOTECHNIK MIT NACHFOLGENDEM ANSCHLAG: Gleiche Technik wie das gebundene Glissando, jedoch wird die zweite Note angeschlagen.

NATÜRLICHES FLAGEOLETT: Berühre die Saite über dem angegebenen Bund leicht mit einem Finger der Griffhand. Schlage die Saite an und lasse sie frei schwingen.

PICK SCRAPE: Fahre mit dem Plektrum nach unten über die Saiten - klappt am besten bei umsponnenen Saiten.

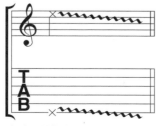

DÄMPFEN MIT DER SCHLAGHAND: Lege die Schlaghand oberhalb der Brücke leicht auf die Saite(n).

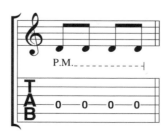

DÄMPFEN MIT DER GRIFFHAND: Du erreichst einen percussiven Sound, indem du die Griffhand leicht über die Saiten legst (ohne diese herunterzudrücken) und dann mit der Schlaghand anschlägst.

AMMERKUNG: Das Tempo der Zieher und Glissandos ist abhängig von der rhythmischen Notation und dem Grundtempo.

Spiegazioni Di Tablatura Per Chitarra

La musica per chitarra può essere annotata in tre diversi modi: sul pentagramma, in tablatura e in taglio ritmico

IL TAGLIO RITMICO è scritto sopra il pentagramma. Percuotere le corde al ritmo indicato Le teste arrotondate delle note indicano note singole.

IL PENTAGRAMMA MUSICALE mostra toni e ritmo ed è divisa da linee in settori. I toni sono indicati con le prime sette lettere dell'alfabeto.

LA TABLATURA rappresenta graficamente la tastiera della chitarra. Ogni linea orizzontale rappresenta una corda, ed ogni corda rappresenta un tasto.

4° corda, 2° tasto   1° e 2° corda aperte, suonate insieme   accordo D aperto

Definizioni Per Annotazioni Speciali Per Chitarra

SEMI-TONO CURVATO: percuotere la nota e curvare di un semitono (1/2 passo).

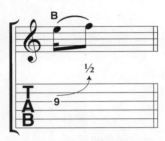

TONO CURVATO: Percuotere la nota e curvare di un tono (passo intero).

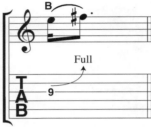

NOTA BREVE, CURVATA: percuotere la nota e curvare come indicato. Suonare la prima nota il più velocemente possibile.

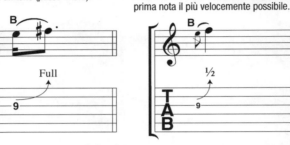

QUARTO DI TONO, CURVATO: Percuotere la nota e curvare di un quarto di passo.

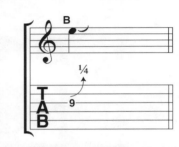

CURVA E LASCIA: Percuotere la nota e curvare come indicato, quindi rilasciare indietro alla nota originale.

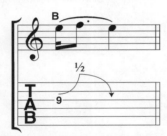

CURVA E RIPERCUOTI: Percuotere la nota e curvare come indicato poi ripercuotere la corda nel punto del simbolo.

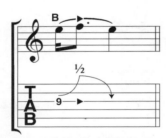

PRE-CURVA: Curvare la nota come indicato e quindi percuoterla.

PRE-CURVA E RILASCIO: Curvare la nota come indicato. Colpire e rilasciare la nota indietro alla tonalità indicata.

MARTELLO-COLPISCI: Colpire la prima nota (in basso) con un dito; quindi suona la nota più alta (sulla stessa corda) con un altro dito, toccandola senza pizzicare.

TOGLIERE: Posizionare entrambe le dita sulla nota da suonare. Colpire la prima nota e, senza pizzicare, togliere le dita per suonare la seconda nota (più in basso).

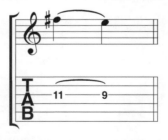

LEGATO SCIVOLATO (GLISSATO): Colpire la prima nota e quindi far scivolare lo stesso dito della mano della tastiera su o giù alla seconda nota. La seconda nota non viene colpita.

CAMBIO SCIVOLATO (GLISSARE E RICOLPIRE): Uguale al legato - scivolato eccetto che viene colpita la seconda nota.

ARMONICA NATURALE: Colpire la nota mentre la mano della tastiera tocca leggermente la corda direttamente sopra il tasto indicato.

PIZZICA E GRAFFIA: Il limite del pizzicato è tirato su (o giù) lungo la corda, producendo un suono graffiante.

SORDINA CON IL PALMO: La nota è parzialmente attenuato dalla mano del pizzicato toccando la corda (le corde) appena prima del ponte.

CORDE SMORZATE: Un suono di percussione viene prodotto appoggiando la mano della tastiera attraverso la corda (le corde) senza premere, e colpendole con la mano del pizzicato.

NOTA: La velocità di ogni curvatura è indicata dalle annotazioni musicali e dal tempo.